CANDY BEAR

ANDY BEAR

A POLAR CUB GROWS UP AT THE ZOO

BY GINNY JOHNSTON & JUDY CUTCHINS

PHOTOGRAPHS BY CONSTANCE NOBLE

DISCARDED

WILLIAM MORROW & CO., INC. · NEW YORK

SCHENECTADY COUNTY
PUBLIC LIBRARY

To Constance Noble,
whose skill in zoo work and love of zoo animals
have earned our wholehearted admiration.

—G.J. AND J.C.

PHOTO CREDITS: All photographs are by Constance Noble with the exception of the following: Judy A. Cutchins, pp. 8, 12, 13, 15-17, 40, 49; Fernbank Science Center (Judy A. Cutchins, photographer), pp. 20, 53; Kathleen Flynn, pp. 14, 21, 35 top, 43 bottom, 48; Russell Porter, pp. 19, 36, 50, 55, 60. Permission is gratefully acknowledged.

Text copyright © 1985 by Ginny Johnston and Judy A. Cutchins

All rights reserved. No part of this book may be reproduced or utilized in any form or by any means, electronic or mechanical, including photocopying, recording or by any information storage and retrieval system, without permission in writing from the Publisher. Inquiries should be addressed to William Morrow and Company, Inc., 105 Madison Avenue, New York, NY 10016. Printed in Hong Kong by South China Printing Company.
Book design by Arlene Goldberg

1 2 3 4 5 6 7 8 9 10

Library of Congress Cataloging in Publication Data
Johnston, Ginny. Andy Bear : a polar cub grows up at the zoo.
Includes index. Summary: Describes the first year of life of a polar bear born in captivity at the Atlanta Zoo. 1. Polar bear—Juvenile literature. 2. Animals, Infancy of—Juvenile literature. 3. Zoo animals—Juvenile literature. [1. Polar bear. 2. Animals—Infancy. 3. Zoo animals] I. Cutchins, Judy. II. Title.
QL737.C27C88   1985   636′.974446   85-3095
ISBN 0-688-05627-X
ISBN 0-688-05628-8 (lib. bdg.)

ACKNOWLEDGMENTS

J 599.74
JOH
C.4

We would like to thank Dr. Terry L. Maple, Director, and Susan Hood, Assistant Director of Operations, of the Atlanta Zoological Park in Atlanta, Georgia, for their expert reading of the manuscript.

—G.J. and J.C.

I wish to thank a number of Atlanta Zoological Park people for their help in raising Andy Bear. First of all, thanks to my longtime friend Ron Jackson, Curator of Mammals. This story is partly his. He is the man behind the scenes holding everything together. Also, thanks to Director Terry Maple and my fellow zookeepers. Special appreciation to my good friend and coworker Ruth Visscher, and to Henry Spratlin, Assistant Curator of Mammals, who taught me to talk to the big cats.

I also gratefully acknowledge my dear friends who took care of me while I took care of Andy. I would never have made it without Lynn and Danny Tipton, Laulie and Charles Naser, Kathleen Flynn, Russell Porter, and Leon Horton.

I wish to recognize Mayor Andrew Young and the Atlanta Parks and Recreation Department, especially Commissioners Carolyn Hatcher and Geri Elder, for their support and for giving me the honor and privilege of raising such a magnificent animal.

I'd like to express sincere appreciation for the advice and professional help of James Rowell, Brookfield Zoo, Columbia, South Carolina; Dr. Jim Melton, and the Small Animal Department of Auburn University Veterinary School, Auburn, Alabama; Dr. M. Silverman, Emory University, Atlanta, Georgia; and Dr. Emmett Ashley, Atlanta, Georgia.

—C.N.

INTRODUCTION

The majestic polar bear lives in the ice-covered Arctic near the North Pole. This sleek, creamy white bear is the largest meat-eating animal that lives on land. A full-grown male reaches 8 feet in length and weighs over 1,000 pounds. The female is smaller but still one of the strongest of all animals.

An adult male polar bear usually wanders alone, but during the spring, the male finds a female for mating. They spend a few days together and then go their separate ways again. The male has no part in raising his cubs. In fact, he will kill and eat them.

In late fall, the pregnant female polar bear digs an igloo-like den in a snowdrift. She dozes as she awaits the birth of her cubs in December or January. Usually the female gives birth to twins, each no bigger than a guinea pig and weighing only a pound or two. The young cubs grow quickly as they nurse on the fat-rich milk of their mother. By late March, each furry cub weighs nearly 25 pounds. Soon, mother and cubs break out of their snow-covered den.

Standing on its hind legs, the adult male polar bear would be eye to eye with an elephant.

Throughout the summer and fall, the growing cubs are never out of the mother's sight. Only 12 inches tall, they follow her closely as she searches for food, taking care not to fall into her enormous footprints in the snow. The mother bear growls and "talks" to her cubs often as she teaches them the ways of the polar bear.

By the end of the summer, the cubs weigh close to 100 pounds each, but they are still closely guarded and fed by their mother. In the fall, the polar bear family may den up again for protection against the harsh winter when temperatures reach forty degrees below zero. After the second year, the cubs leave their mother to explore the icy Arctic world alone.

Polar bears have been hunted for hundreds of years. Fifteen years ago, scientists began to study the great white bears in the Arctic. They estimated 20,000 polar bears were living there, but each year too many were being killed by hunters. In 1972, a law was passed in America to protect the polar bears. Four years later, an international agreement was signed by all the Arctic nations to limit the number of polar bears that could be killed each year. Now, the big bear is out of serious danger from hunters.

But the polar bear habitat is in danger from hunters of a different kind. People who are searching for oil and minerals beneath the Arctic ice threaten to destroy the polar bears' environment. Much more must be learned about the polar bears and their way of life in order to protect them.

Some zoos around the world are trying to help find out more about polar bears. They are breeding these beautiful animals in captivity and studying their habits. However, because people still know so little about the needs of polar bears, raising newborn cubs in zoos is very difficult. Most polar bear cubs in captivity do not survive.

Constance Noble in Atlanta, Georgia, is one of very few zookeepers in the world who has succeeded in keeping polar bear cubs alive. *Andy Bear* is the story of Constance and one of these rare cubs.

Andrew Nicholas Polar Bear

ANDY BEAR

It was ten-thirty on Christmas morning and the Atlanta Zoo was closed to visitors. But, to the animals, Christmas was just like any other day. They were hungry and needed attention.

Most of the zookeepers had finished their work and gone home for the day. Only Constance Noble and one other keeper were still working. Constance loved her work at the zoo. She had cared for lions, bobcats, monkeys, sea lions, and bears for more than ten years. The animals seemed to know she was their friend.

"What a warm morning for December," Constance thought as she walked along the zookeeper's pathway behind the bear cages.

Grizzlies, Asiatic black bears, Malayan sun bears, Kodiaks, and polar bears all lived at the zoo. Each kind of bear had a cage with both indoor and outdoor areas. Inside each cage were two small "dens." These cavelike rooms allowed the bears some peace and quiet away from crowds of visitors. One of the dens in each cage opened

11

Constance cleans the cage for Alice, an African lion.

into an outside yard with a swimming pool. In the yard the bears could exercise or sleep in the sunshine while visitors watched.

Climbing the ladder behind the polar bears' cage, Constance looked over the high rock wall into the yard below. She saw only Thor, the 1200-pound male bear, sleeping comfortably in the yard. Linda, the female polar bear, was inside the den. The two Siberian polar bears had shared a cage at the zoo for almost twenty years. Zookeepers had placed them together as playmates when they were very young. In the wild, male bears are loners, rarely having any contact with females. At the zoo, Thor and Linda have developed an unusual polar bear relationship because they are constant companions.

In their cage, the sliding metal door between the inside dens and the outside yard was open so the bears could go in or out as they pleased. Constance tossed two pounds of

Thor sleeps late on winter mornings.

The enormous Kodiak bear waits to be fed.

chunky, dry food called "bear chow" into the yard. Seeing nothing unusual, she climbed down and went next door to feed the grizzlies, then the Kodiaks.

Just as she was finishing her work at the Kodiaks' cage, the quiet of the Christmas morning was shattered by ear-splitting screams and frightening howls. These terrifying sounds were coming from the polar bears!

Constance rushed behind the cages and looked through a small back door into the polar bears' den. She could see Thor. His head was lowered and he was snorting fiercely as he tried to come into the den. Inside, Linda was moaning and howling as she blocked the doorway with her 700-pound body. The screams were coming from a corner inside the dark den.

Constance knew immediately what was happening. During the night Linda had given birth to a cub and was protecting it from the powerful Thor. Now that he was awake, the father bear, with his extraordinary sense of smell, had discovered the new cub inside the den. If Thor got to the baby he would kill it.

A male polar bear will kill any newcomer, even his own cub. In the Arctic, polar bear mothers and newborn cubs live beneath the snow in large dens safely hidden from the male bears for several months. But, here at the zoo it was different. Zookeepers were afraid to move Thor away from Linda. She might be so lonely and upset she would not take care of her cub.

Thor smells the newborn cub and tries to come into the den.

If Constance throws bear chow over the wall, Linda might go into the yard with Thor.

The only way the baby bear could survive was for Constance to rescue it quickly. For the past few years, all of Linda's cubs had been killed before the zookeepers could get to them.

Constance knew how dangerous polar bears could be, especially at a time like this. These enormous white bears have more strength than gorillas. Constance would be killed if she went inside the den now. Somehow, she had to drive both bears out into the yard. Then she could close the sliding den door, lock them out, and go safely into the den. But how could she force them out?

Grabbing a bucket of bear chow, she rushed up the ladder and threw the food over the wall, hoping to attract Thor and Linda into the yard. It didn't work.

Hurrying down the ladder, she snatched up the hose and sprayed water through an opening in the door. But the bears didn't budge. They stood face to face, Thor growling, Linda moaning, and from deep inside the den, the newborn cub screaming.

Constance, a quiet and gentle zookeeper, was becoming desperate. She knew she was running out of time. Although Linda snapped and growled at Thor, she could not keep him away from the cub much longer. Constance tried the last thing she could think of—she threw a screaming fit! She yelled at the bears, waved her arms, and banged on the door of the cage.

Thor was so surprised he backed out of the doorway. The startled Linda followed him into the yard. Constance couldn't believe her eyes. Quickly she ran to pull the

To rescue the cub, Constance locks Thor
and Linda in the outside yard.

17

handle that closed the den's sliding door. Both adult polar bears were locked out. At last, the cub would be safe.

Constance unlocked the zookeeper's doorway and crawled into the den. She stood up slowly and squinted in the darkness. At first she couldn't see anything. The cub was quiet now, making it even harder to find. Constance shuffled her feet along the floor hoping not to step on the baby. When her foot bumped into the cub, it began to scream again. As her eyes adjusted to the dimness of the den, Constance could just about see the shape of the cub. It was no bigger than a guinea pig. She picked it up, gently snuggling its warm body to her chest, and headed for the zoo clinic.

By the time she arrived at the clinic, the cub was quiet. Constance examined the baby. It was a perfectly healthy boy!

The newborn cub is the size of a guinea pig.

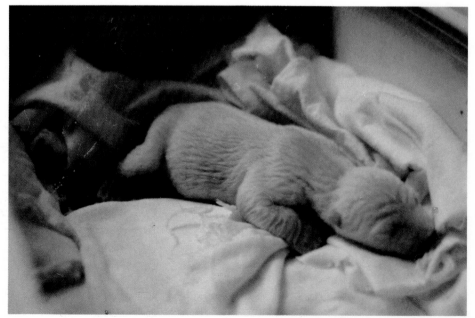

The zookeepers had decided to name the next male cub born at the zoo Andrew, in honor of the city's mayor, Andrew Young. Later they gave the tiny cub a middle name, Nicholas, because he was born on Christmas morning. Andrew Nicholas Polar Bear was called Andy for short.

Andy weighed just under 1½ pounds. He had a pink nose and his tiny ears were flat against his head. His eyes were closed and his wrinkled, pink body was covered with fine, white fur. Although Andy could already hold his head up, it would be weeks before he could walk.

Constance placed Andy in an incubator where he would be safe and warm. She made a formula of evaporated milk and water. Every hour and a half, she squirted a little of the mixture into Andy's mouth.

Andy sucks on Constance's finger as she gently squirts the milk formula into his mouth.

While the other zookeeper watched Andy, Constance left the clinic just long enough to check on Thor and Linda. Thor was resting quietly now on a large rock in the yard. But Linda was moaning and pacing around. She didn't understand why her cub was gone. Constance wished she could explain to the lonely mother bear that this was the only way her cub could survive at the zoo.

Zoo officials were excited about the birth of Andy and the miraculous rescue by Constance. They knew this rare baby polar bear would need attention twenty-four hours a day. Constance was placed in charge of the new cub. Since she could not live at the small zoo clinic, Constance took Andy home with her. While Constance cared for

After the excitement, Thor rests quietly on a rock.

Linda misses her cub.

Andy at her apartment, another zookeeper would do her zoo chores until she returned.

For the next few months, Constance would have to become a mother polar bear—comforting, warming, and feeding the baby bear night and day. Constance knew that the biggest problem would be mixing a formula identical to real polar bear milk. The milk of the mother polar bear is very different from any milk Constance could buy. It is much thicker and creamier.

Constance watched Andy closely and kept a diary of each change in the little bear as he grew. When Andy

21

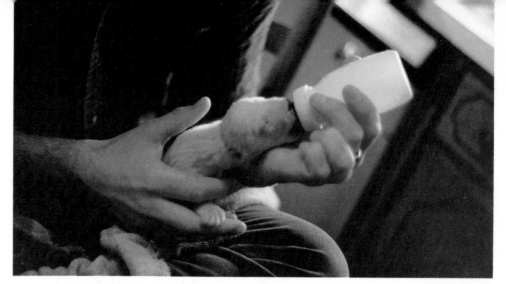
Constance has to feed Andy every 1½ hours.

was just three days old, Constance noticed that his soft, pink nose and pink foot pads were starting to turn black. This was good news; it meant the cub was growing normally. She was still feeding him every hour and a half. After the first week, Andy had gained one pound. Now, he weighed 2½ pounds!

One stormy evening, Constance sat in her bedroom jotting notes in her diary about Andy's tenth day. Nearby, Andy was crawling around in his playpen. He couldn't walk yet, because his little legs would not hold him up. Suddenly, a flash of lightning and a crash of thunder startled the bear cub, and he began to cry.

Over the next few days, Constance noticed that Andy was very sensitive to loud noises. The ring of the telephone scared him and caused him to whimper. Constance asked her friends not to call. She stopped using her noisy dishwasher. Even the television and radio had to be turned down so low they could hardly be heard.

Andy was changing in other ways, too. When he was twenty-eight days old, his shiny, dark eyes opened for the first time. Thicker fur was beginning to cover his body.

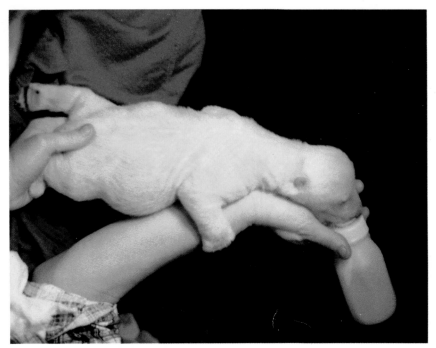

*The little cub changes as he grows. At one
week, Andy weighs 2½ pounds . . .*

and when he is four weeks old, his eyes open.

Constance had been working so hard, she had not had time to notice what a beautiful animal little Andrew Nicholas was becoming. He was less like a furry ball and more like a polar bear. He was developing the long muscular neck that makes polar bears look so different from other bears.

Although the first four weeks had not been easy, the next four were even harder. By the end of January, Andy was becoming very sick. Just as Constance had feared, the milk formula was the cause of his problems. His delicate digestive system was not working properly. Constance knew if Andy got any sicker, he could die. Polar cubs are so rare in captivity that neither Constance nor the zoo veterinarian knew exactly what to do for Andy. They tried several "people" medicines, hoping to find the one that would save Andy's life.

After one month, Andy gets sick.

To make matters worse, Andy was cutting his baby teeth, and his gums were very sore. The doctor gave him mild painkillers to make the teething easier. Constance wondered how this tiny bear that weighed just 5 pounds could possibly survive. It seemed hopeless, but she would not give up.

Hour after hour, day after day, Constance sat with the sick little bear until the medicines finally began to work. Andy at last rested more comfortably. Constance was using a different formula consisting of cream and water, and Andy was feeling much better. His digestive problems were finally over and his baby teeth were all in place. By the last week in February, Constance could relax a little. Now two months old, Andy was gaining weight again, and his eyes were shining brightly.

He finally begins to get stronger and feel better as the medicine begins to work.

Healthy and curious, the polar cub is eager to explore, indoors . . .

and out.

Constance watched one morning as Andy stretched, yawned, and rolled onto his stomach after a long nap. On unsteady but determined legs, he took his first steps.

Andy bites everything within reach with his sharp teeth.

Nine-week-old Andy was walking! Now Constance would have to watch him even more closely.

Andy began to suck on everything he came near. He

sucked on his blanket and on Constance's arm. His sharp little teeth caused a painful bite, but when she pulled away, Andy screamed. Constance solved the problem by giving Andy a baby bottle nipple to use as a pacifier.

One afternoon in late March, Constance sat relaxing by her window watching a rare southern snowfall gently cover the ground. She decided to give Andy a taste of what "real" Arctic polar bear life might be like.

She bundled herself up with a coat and gloves and opened the back door. Andy stepped uncertainly onto the soft white blanket of snow. Suddenly, out he went! He looked like a running, sliding snowball of fur. A squirrel

Andy Bear romps in his first real snow.

*Sometimes Constance lets her friends hold
Andy for a few minutes.*

scurried to the warmth of its nearby nest. Constance
knew Andy wouldn't be cold because polar bears have
thick fur and layers of fat to keep them warm. Even the
bottoms of their feet are covered with fur. In the Arctic,
temperatures drop to forty degrees below zero.

Constance and her friends enjoyed romping with Andy
Bear, but they were always careful of the frisky cub's
teeth. Constance had already lost a fingernail because of
his powerful bite. Even three-month-old polar bears have
very strong jaws. Constance knew that although she had

Andy "helps"
Constance with
her flower
garden.

Andy Bear thinks he's found a playmate in the mirror.

rescued Andy and raised him from a tiny cub, he was not a pet. In just a few months he would weigh over 100 pounds and be a strong and unpredictable polar bear.

By spring, Andy was becoming more curious and playful. He climbed on the kitchen counters and chewed on the furniture. Andy was wrecking Constance's apartment. Outdoors, he splashed in the water, dug in the garden, and explored in the yard. At 25 pounds, Andy was becoming a problem around the house. His claws were over an inch long and his teeth were very sharp. It was time for Andy to return to the zoo.

Zookeepers built a large, roomy wooden pen inside the zoo clinic. Moving him to this new indoor cage frightened

Andy snuggles with his favorite blankets in his new cage in the clinic.

and upset him. Constance tried to make the move easy for Andy. She filled the pen with his toys. Most importantly, she placed his favorite blankets in the new pen to make him feel at home.

Constance stayed at the clinic with Andy many hours each day. While she was there, she worked and played with Charlie Bob. He was a tame bobcat that, like Andy, had been raised by Constance.

Late at night, when she went home for a few hours of sleep, Andy cried. Constance knew that Andy thought of her as his "mother" bear. And, in the wild, mother bears are with their cubs every minute.

Each morning at five-thirty, Constance returned to the clinic and Andy was very happy to see her. The hungry little bear was ready for his breakfast of strained beef mixed into five bottles of milk. Constance also fed him oatmeal, chopped apples, and cooked carrots. Andy was eating this meal six times a day now.

Sometimes Constance let Andy out of his pen in the clinic. He soon made friends with Charlie Bob. Andy got to know other zookeepers who stopped by the clinic. They let him out of his pen to explore, but Andy was never left alone. As Constance and her friends looked on, Andy climbed on chairs and desks. He poked his head into drawers and buckets. Andy Bear was into everything!

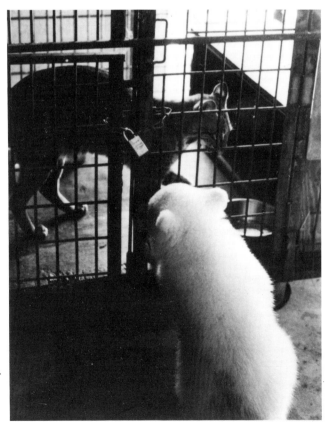

The little polar bear cub makes friends with Charlie Bob.

In the clinic, Andy Bear is into everything.
He loves to climb on chairs whenever he is
out of his pen . . .

and to shred cardboard
boxes with his sharp teeth.

Sometimes Constance took her little bear friend out with her as she made her rounds to feed the other animals and to clean their cages. It was a good way for Andy to get the exercise he needed while Constance worked.

She taught Andy a few commands. He was very smart and quickly understood her tone of voice when she firmly told him, "No!" He also learned what to do when she said, "Lie down."

The little polar bear follows Constance outside . . .

and learns to "stay" on command.

One day, Andy was romping with Constance behind the sea lions' pen. Suddenly, one of the largest sea lions barked at him. The cub ran away as fast as his little legs would carry him. He tripped over a brick and fell sprawling to the ground. Constance rushed to the crying baby. His front leg seemed to be injured. She carried him back to the clinic where the zoo veterinarian X-rayed the leg. The doctor said the leg was broken. Andy would have to be taken to a special animal hospital one hundred miles away.

It was getting late. Constance offered to stay at the zoo clinic with Andy until morning. Then they would make the long trip to the hospital.

Although the veterinarian had given the cub some-

A serious fall breaks Andy's front leg.

An injured Andy snuggles close to Constance.

thing to make him feel better, the night was a sleepless one for Andy and Constance. Andy rested his head against Constance's knee. She knew his cries and whimpers were the sounds of a frightened and hurting little bear. "It's going to be all right, Andy. The doctors will fix you up," Constance whispered as she petted him soothingly. She cared very much for the little cub she had mothered for the past four months.

At the hospital, the doctors gave Andy medicine to calm him and to make his leg stop hurting. They shaved

*At the animal hospital, the cub waits for
the doctors.*

the fur from Andy's broken leg. Then they operated on
the leg to insert a metal pin that would hold the broken
bone together.

Constance took Andy back to the zoo. In just a few days
he could walk on his injured leg. For the next four weeks,
Constance watched over him carefully. Then she took
him back to the animal hospital. The doctors checked the
leg and removed the pin. Andy was as good as new.

Constance looks into the cage to check on
Andy's stitches.

Even with a broken leg, the growing cub
never loses his appetite.

By the middle of May, Andrew Nicholas was almost five months old and weighed 55 pounds. He was getting too big and too strong to run around inside the clinic.

Constance realized it was time for the little polar cub to live outside in a larger zoo cage. The zookeepers were afraid to put Andy into the cage with Thor and Linda. The adult bears might not accept the cub. If they didn't, they would kill Andy. All the other bear cages were full, so the zookeepers cleaned out a large, round cage near the sea lion house for Andy.

Just after dawn, while the zoo was still quiet and no workmen or noisy trucks were around to frighten Andy, Constance arrived to take him to his new home. She let Andy out of his playpen; then she opened the clinic door and led the cub outside. He trusted Constance and fol-

Constance leads Andy to his new outdoor cage.

lowed closely on her heels as she led him across the grassy lawn and into his new cage.

Curious Andy was fascinated by this new place. While Constance stayed in the cage with him, Andy explored every inch. Constance put two of Andy's favorite blankets in the little rock den, hoping Andy would sleep there. Andy splashed in the shallow pool of water. Constance was relieved and delighted because he seemed to feel right at home.

Andy has fun splashing in the shallow pool.

*Andy watches
Constance as she
opens the cage door.*

    After an hour, Constance opened the door and stepped
out of the cage. Andy looked up and ran to follow her. He
did not want her to leave. When Constance locked the
door, Andy cried. The farther away Constance walked,
the louder and more terrified Andy's cries became.

The frightened cub rushes to follow Constance as she leaves the cage . . .

but her reassuring voice calms him.

Returning to the cage, Constance reached through the bars to pet the upset cub. She whispered reassuringly, "Don't be afraid, Andy, I won't be far away." The cries stopped, and he lay down with his head against the bars as close to Constance as he could get.

As Constance stroked his thick fur, Andy sucked on his pacifier and began his purring noises. He had been making

Andy Bear purrs contentedly with his pacifier.

A frightened Andy screams for Constance.

this sound since he was three months old. Constance called it "motorboating" because it sounded like a motorboat. She knew when he did this he was no longer upset.

Constance started away from the cage again, but Andy began to whimper. She couldn't leave him alone. By seven that night, the exhausted little bear finally went to sleep. Constance sat on the wall beside his cage for a little while longer. She was tired from the long day with Andy and hoped by the next morning he would be used to his new surroundings.

Back at her apartment, Constance worried all night about Andy. Early the next morning, after very little sleep, she drove to the zoo. Andy was not only wide-awake, he was screaming! She could hear him when she drove into the parking lot. Running toward the cage, Constance feared Andy might be hurt. When she reached him, he quieted down. Constance realized Andy was not hurt at all. The cub was upset because he had spent a lonely and frightened first night in his outdoor cage.

Constance decided she would stay beside Andy's cage all day and part of the night for the rest of the week. "Surely," she thought, "Andy will be settled into his new home by then."

Nighttime was the biggest problem for Andy. Lights and noises from cars awakened and frightened him. These were all new and fearful experiences for the cub that had spent all his young life safely protected indoors.

By midsummer, Constance was still spending long days and evenings sitting on the wall beside Andy's cage. A wooden fence had been built on one side of the cage to block the car lights from Andy's view. This made nights a little less terrifying for the cub. Constance talked to Andy, petted, and fed him.

Although he was often upset, the growing cub had a very good appetite. He was eating only four or five times a day now, but he was getting three pounds of strained beef, six bottles of milk, and a handful of bear chow at each feeding. Andy wanted all the food that he saw or smelled.

Between feedings he sucked on his pacifier and motor-boated. He was quiet and content as long as Constance was nearby. Andy Bear was a big, fluffy, 100-pound polar cub now, but a baby just the same.

As days went by, Constance found she could get away to do other zoo chores while Andy slept. But Andy was never left alone. Another zookeeper stayed with him

The hungry cub drinks dozens of bottles of milk each day.

Andy sits comfortably surrounded by his blankets.

*Thousands of summer visitors are delighted
by the antics of the cub.*

when Constance was gone. Life for the polar bear cub
was finally becoming easier in his new home. Andy began to enjoy visitors and he played with his basketball
and swinging tire. He chewed on his blankets until they
were in shreds. Constance gave him her tennis shoes and
socks. The cub tossed them around the cage and chewed
them to pieces.

Stories about Andy Bear's miraculous survival had
been reported on television and in the newspapers and

magazines all over the United States. He had thousands of visitors that summer. Some people returned week after week to watch the little bear grow. Even the mayor Andy was named after came by to see the cub.

By the end of the summer, Andy was twice as big as he had been in May, but he was still drinking milk from baby bottles. Constance usually gave him two at a time. In fact, he loved the bottle so much that he wanted every one he saw. He whined and jumped up and down whenever visitors strolled by with babies holding bottles. Andy wanted their bottles, too! Many people gave bottles, stuffed animals, and other toys to the special little white bear.

Of all the visitors, Smokey was Andy's favorite. He

Smokey, the manager of the zoo's refreshment stands, is one of Andy's favorite visitors.

was the manager of the zoo's refreshment stands. Every day, Smokey would drive his scooter around to open all the stands and deliver ice. One hot summer day, Smokey stopped at Andy's cage and gave him a snow cone. Andy loved the cold, slushy treat. When Smokey drove by the next day, Andy bounced up and down and banged on his cage. Smokey stopped his scooter and gave him another snow cone. After that, Andy bounced up and down each morning to get Smokey's attention. And he always got a fresh, icy treat from his new friend.

One day Smokey brought Andy a whole bucket of

Ice is a delightful treat on a hot summer day.

crushed ice. Andy was crazy about it. He rolled in the pile of slush and rubbed it with his paws. Watching the little bear, Constance commented to some visitors that it would be great if Andy had his own ice machine. One of the visitors called a newspaper reporter who wrote a short story that appeared in the paper the next day. It explained Andrew Nicholas's love for ice. That same day, someone read the article and sent Andy his very own ice machine.

Fat, furry Andy will not be cold during the winter.

Constance was amazed at how quickly the summer passed by. Like polar bears in the Arctic, Andy had been storing up body fat throughout the warm summer months. This layer of fat would keep Andy comfortable during the winter.

Thanksgiving Day found Constance and Andy alone at the zoo. Some friends surprised her with a turkey dinner. Of course, Andy was invited to share in the feast. He ate turkey, dressing, and cranberry sauce. Then he pulled the tablecloth into his cage and chewed it to bits!

Early in December, Constance began to watch Linda carefully. It was time for another cub to be born.

One Sunday night as Constance sat near Andy's cage, she heard Thor and Linda fighting. Constance knew the only time the two adult polar bears ever fought was when a cub was born. She rushed to their cage. This time the rescue was easy. Both Thor and Linda were already in the outside yard. Constance locked them out and

Thor and Linda only fight when a cub is born.

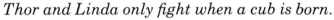

crawled into the den. She quickly picked up the newborn cub and took it to the clinic. Andy had a new little sister!

Another zookeeper was assigned to help Constance with the new baby. Raising the cub at the clinic would mean Constance would still be able to spend a few hours each day with Andy.

Soon Christmas came and Andy had his first birthday. "You certainly have changed," said Constance as she petted her friend and remembered when he was as tiny as his new sister. Now Andy weighed almost 150 pounds! Constance would not be able to reach into his cage much longer. Even in play, Andy's strong jaws and sharp claws could be extremely dangerous.

The year-old polar bear cub has very sharp claws . . .

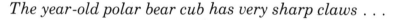

and now weighs 150 pounds.

A large, deep pool is built in Andy's permanent cage.

Workers were preparing a bigger and better outdoor cage for Andy next door to the grizzlies. They built a large swimming pool in Andy's outdoor yard. After weeks of work, the cage was ready.

To move Andy, the zookeepers brought a narrow, rolling cage up to his door. Constance held an ice cream cone through the bars and coaxed the cub inside. As the cage was carefully rolled across the zoo yard, Andy cried and jumped up and down. Constance walked close to the frightened cub and spoke to him over and over as the cage was moved. The sound of her voice was reassuring to the young bear. Another zookeeper went ahead to move Andy's toys.

In a few minutes they were at Andy's new den door. The rolling cage was opened and he stepped into his new home. Running through the den and into the outside yard, Andy spotted some of his favorite toys.

Andy paced nervously around the yard, and Constance stayed near his den door all day. She was prepared to stay all night, but Andy surprised her. By nine o'clock he was sound asleep with his blankets inside the large, cave-like den. Andy seemed to feel safe there.

The frightened cub paces nervously in the narrow rolling cage.

Andy Bear seems afraid to jump into the deep pool . . .

but like all polar bears, he loves the water.

The next day he looked like he was right at home. Constance watched the curious bear explore his new cage. He tested the water in the pool with his nose and paws. Twice he fell in and came scrambling out as fast as he could. Constance was amazed that Andy seemed to be afraid of the deep water. Polar bears with their webbed front feet are excellent swimmers. By the end of the second week, however, Andy had discovered that playing in the pool was fun.

Constance was spending less time every day near Andy's cage. Andy was really growing up. Constance smiled at her little friend as she turned away thinking, "He's going to be just fine."

At last, Andy Bear is a healthy, well-adjusted zoo bear.

Constance's friend cares for Snowball in the zoo clinic.

She headed for the zoo clinic, where Snowball, Andy's little sister, was being cared for by another zookeeper. As she entered the clinic and looked at the tiny cub, Constance remembered how difficult the first months of Andy's life had been. Once he had nearly died, and now he was a strong, healthy, and well-adjusted zoo bear. Constance had learned many things from her year with Andy. She hoped her experience would make raising another rare polar cub easier.

INDEX